Ina's Kitchen

ONE INA

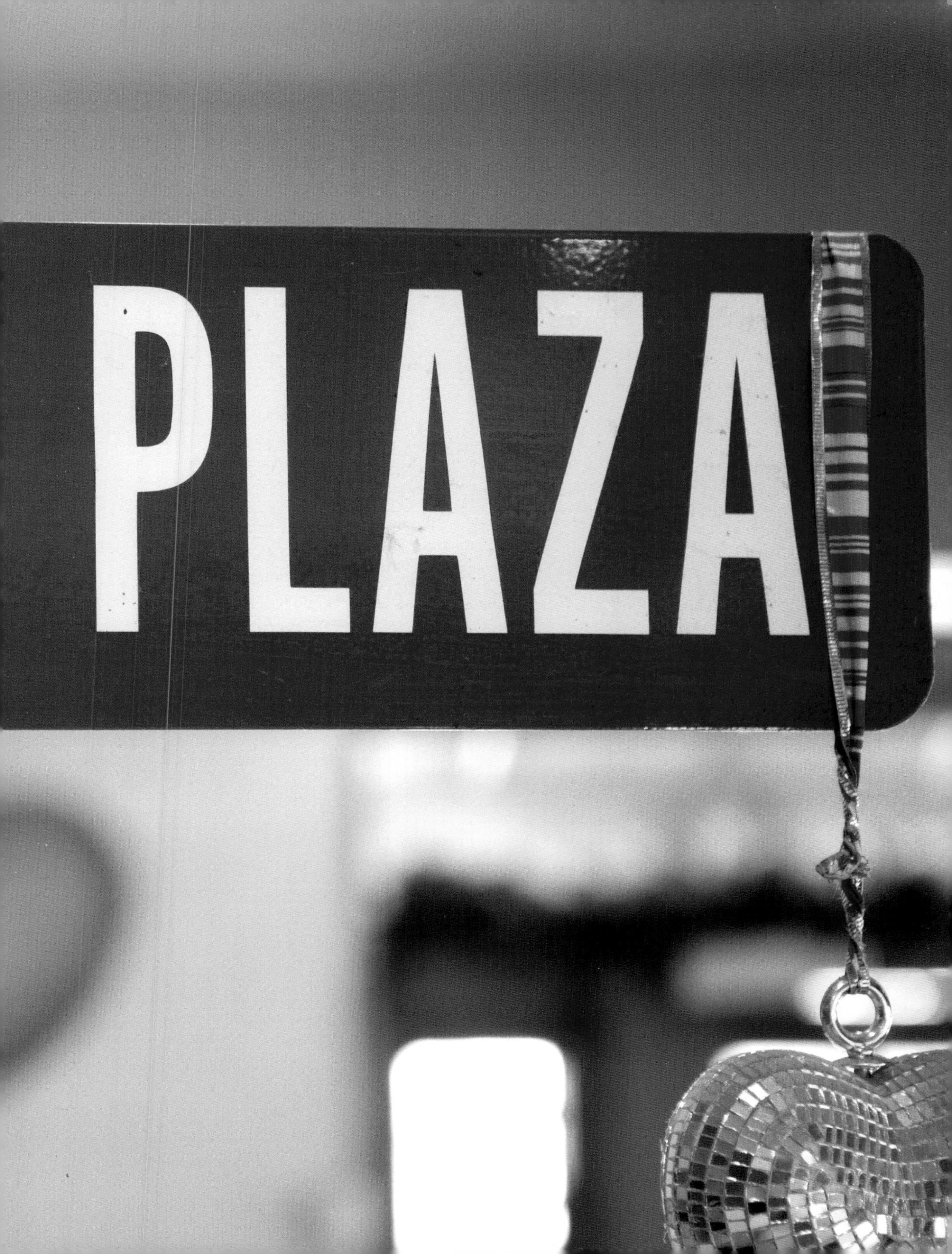
PLAZA

I dedicate this book to my father and champion,
Steve Brody, who always said,
"I have confidence in you!"
and
Seana Monahan, the embodiment of intelligence,
commitment, compassion, loyalty and love.

♥

Ina's Kitchen

MEMORIES AND RECIPES FROM THE BREAKFAST QUEEN

by Ina Pinkney

Photography by Stephen Hamilton

Design by Christina Silvestris

MIDWAY

AN AGATE IMPRINT

CHICAGO

Copyright © 2013, 2015 by Ina Pinkney

Design by Christina Silvestris
All photography copyright © Stephen Hamilton

Printed in China

Library of Congress Cataloging-in-Publication Data

Pinkney, Ina
 Ina's Kitchen : memories and recipes from the Breakfast Queen / Ina Pinkney.
    pages cm
 Summary: "Memoir and recipes from the owner of Chicago restaurant Ina's Kitchen"--Provided by publisher.
 Includes bibliographical references.
 ISBN 978-1-57284-181-9 (pbk.) -- ISBN 1-57284-181-8 (pbk.) -- ISBN 978-1-57284-766-8 (ebook) -- ISBN 1-57284-766-2 (ebook)
 1. Breakfasts. 2. Ina's Kitchen (Chicago, Ill.) I. Title.
 TX733.P636 2013
 641.5'2--dc23
                              2015013583

10 9 8 7 6 5 4 3 2 1

Midway is an imprint of Agate Publishing. Agate books are available in bulk at discount prices. For more information, go to agatepublishing.com.

table of contents

CHAPTER FOUR: *SERVE AND ENJOY*

CHAPTER FIVE: *CLEAN UP*

INA'S RECIPES

table of contents

THE DESSERT KITCHEN RECIPES

Acknowledgments

When guests ask, "Are you Ina?" I always say,
"Yes... and it's good to be INA!"

It gets a laugh and while it's a great ice-breaker and
gives them a sense of who we are, it's the truest thing
I've ever said.

I have been feeding Chicago for over 30 years but it
wouldn't have happened without 'TEAM INA' behind
me every step of the way.

Most of these names won't mean much or anything
to most of you, but there was never more truth to the
words, "I couldn't have done it without you,"
because each one of you made it possible for me to
say my 'opening line.'

Thank you to:

My FFH (Fabulous Former Husband) Bill Pinkney,
Anne Koch, Barbara Ruben, Dan Rosenthal, Glenn
Alexander, Lloyd Barber and Dick Brown, Jimmy
Bannos, Trinity Bills, Eleanor Binstock, Fern Bogot,
Tim Burton, Steve Dolinsky, Joan Elias, Dima Elissa,
Jeri Elliott, Monica Eng, Michelle Farrell, Elaine
Farrell, Chef Gale Gand, Jim and Diana Gleichman,
Bill Goddu and Paul Osgood, John Herrera, Joan
Hersh, Mary Abbott Hess, Judith Hines, Chris
Holinger, Francine and Alan Inbinder, Paul Kahan,

Donnie Madia and the loving PQM staff, Matt Kirouac, Chris Lackner, Antonia Lortis, Miae Lim, Noeleen McGrath, Rich Melman and my mentors at LEYE, Henedine Monahan, Daniel Ng, Bill O'Donnell, John Panagakos, Sam Rosen, Sal Ruggiero, Debbie Sharpe, Kantha Shelke, Tara Shelke, Chef Art Smith, Michael Sneed, Pat and John Sondergoth, the great staff at SMOQUE, Anne Spiselman, Marylou and Richard Stern, Claudia Sutherland Penella, David Tamarkin, Frank Thomas, Bob Turek, Phil Vettel, Ken Weiner, Andrew Weithe, Carole Widmayer, Elizabeth Wiley, Robin Wold, Lizzie and Mark Zebro.

I owe so much to the staff that has been with me for years and made each day possible.
Thank you to my core team..... Roberto Ortiz, Fausto Jara, Robin Larrea, Jose Cruz, Martin Moreno and Jennifer Sandoval.

A VERY special thanks to Paula Galbraith and Barry Sorkin.

There would be no book without Steve Hamilton and his dedicated team, Cece Campise and our Christina Silvestris.

My deepest gratitude and thanks goes to Edith Taber who helped me understand that I really could fly.

Recipe for life:

Life is like baking a cake.
It's raw for a really long time,
it's perfectly baked for a short
time and it's overbaked forever.

Every recipe I write is a short story with a happy ending.

I wish I had had a mother or grandmother who had carefully written down heirloom recipes that I would later treasure. But they both hated to cook!

My Aunt Susie was an instinctive cook with a remarkable palate who never thought to document her lasagna or any of her other dishes, made over and over to get the taste 'just right.'

I suppose musicians see their lives as musical notes on lined paper, artists as colors on a palate, and engineers as a schematic. Mine is a recipe. It has evolved, changed and had adjustments made to it. I've tried over and over to 'get it just right' and when it was finally perfect, I made notes on it so I could replicate and share it. It's the same with my recipes for breakfast.

Ask people about breakfast and they'll tell you it's their favorite meal. Ask them what they eat at home for breakfast and they'll hesitate, look embarrassed and tell you they eat Pop-Tarts, energy bars, diet cola or juice.

Ask them about eating breakfast in a restaurant, however, and they'll light up and tell an entirely different story about steel cut oatmeal, baked french toast and waffles!

What is it about that specific meal eaten in a restaurant? It has the aura of a special occasion, out of the ordinary routine and what you do on vacation.

There is a lot of mediocre food served at breakfast and I have a theory about that.

At home, when you attempt this meal, you're in the kitchen making each part separately and bringing dish after dish to the table, going back for the next items one by one until you sit down to your cold eggs.

Sitting at a table in a restaurant, the juice is cold, the coffee steaming, and all the food is served together, hot. People accept poor quality as a trade-off for all that.

So what happens if you take the reason for eating out and add superb food and service to the experience? You get INA'S.

After over 30 years in the food business, I am now considered the 'family cook' for thousands of families.

Weddings, births, family celebrations and even deaths have become part of our legacy. Children I fed years ago are now having children and we eagerly await their 'First Pancake Day.'

People bring memories of their visits to INA'S, assured that the Heavenly Hots they have today will be exactly the same as they were in 1991. (They tell me it's like hearing a favorite song on the radio. You know the words and music and still love hearing it played every time!) We have great admiration for the new and innovative, but we respect consistency and tradition even more.

The stories of my life, which lead to these recipes, are all, in essence, happy ones. I have overcome paralytic polio, danced with Fred Astaire, fed Julia Child, skied on a glacier and gone skydiving. And now I write this book.

These stories live in my heart and I will tell them from that place. Some will make you laugh, some will inspire, some will make you wonder, but all of them will have a happy ending.

Now YOU become MY family, to whom I leave my recipes for life and breakfast.

There are definite steps when attempting a recipe that will help insure its success. First you have to read it carefully. Then you make a plan to determine what you will need before you shop for the ingredients. Preparation may require weighing and measuring, cutting and slicing, dicing and shredding. Cooking is the magical part. Add heat, stir or simmer, boil or bake and it's ready. Present the food. Eat alone over the sink or at a beautifully set table and enjoy the results.

Then clean up.

My life story can be told in that format as well. The INGREDIENTS were family, neighborhood, events and education which led to the PREPARATION. These stories are about choices, learning from experience about what to do and what not to do. It was a time of observation and integration of what I saw and learned. COOKING stories begin to clarify who I would become and how I would proceed. When I got to COOKING, it was having experiences with and about food and restaurants that honed my skills as a baker, chef and entrepreneur. SERVE AND ENJOY is surely INA'S where everything I learned helped me create a magical place. The CLEAN UP section is about working hard to stay on top until the day it's time to move on.

chapter one
Ingredients

From brooklyn to breakfast

My mother hated to cook. I loved to eat.
You can see where this is going.

I remember lots of broiled meats, roasted chickens,
canned vegetables and wedges of iceberg lettuce.
Everything in large quantities. (The butcher thought
we were a family of 8, not 4.) Since we kept a Kosher
home, on 'dairy' nights, there were salmon
croquettes and chocolate pudding.

And, actually, I thought it was all just fine. Until I ate
lasagna at Aunt Susie's house. Meat AND Dairy in
the same dish!?!?!?!? Nirvana.

I heard a saying that you 'can't miss what you can't
measure' and so I got out a 'culinary yardstick' and
decided to find out just what I had been missing.
I read cookbooks, cooking magazines, shared
recipes and visited restaurants with friends.
Learning about food became my hobby.

Little did I guess that my journey would have its
roots way back then. However, it was not a straight
path! I had 21 jobs in 25 years before I found my true
calling and earned the title of The Breakfast Queen.

Recipe for life:

It's better to have a small piece
of something real than a big
piece of something fake.

Daddy = ice cream

Ice cream was one of the basic food groups growing up. My father used to say, when I snubbed my nose at his pistachio over my chocolate, "Ina, there's no such thing as bad ice cream."

One of my most delicious memories happened one snowy night when I was about 8 and was the first time I was allowed to stay up late. My mother wanted ice cream and my father asked if I wanted to go with him. Did I ever! Going out 'in the dark' on a mission to get ice cream made me giddy and grown up all at the same time.

We brought home 'frappes,' as they were called in Brooklyn.

We each had one tall round white container that held the ice cream, a smaller one with the hot fudge and another with whipped cream and the cherry.

We assembled our late night treat and ate. I remember being very still and focused on every sensation, knowing this was a really special occasion.

My guilt over my 6 year old brother asleep in his bed, not getting ice cream, however, made me collect and stack the containers and bury them in the trash so he wouldn't see them in the morning and feel left out.

Until the night he died, my father was the best company, especially over a bowl of ice cream.

Pistachio Ice Cream

pistachio ice cream

1 c.	Unsalted shelled pistachios
¾ c.	Sugar, divided
2 c.	Milk (do not use low-fat or nonfat)
½ tsp.	Almond extract
4	Large egg yolks
1 c.	Whipping cream
¾ c.	Unsalted shelled pistachios, toasted, coarsely chopped

PREPARATION

💜 Finely grind 1 c. pistachios and ¼ c. sugar in processor.

💜 Bring milk and ground pistachio mixture to boil in heavy large saucepan. Remove from heat. Mix in almond extract.

💜 Whisk egg yolks and remaining ½ c. sugar in medium bowl. Gradually whisk in hot milk mixture.

💜 Return custard to saucepan. Cook over low heat until custard thickens and leaves path on back of spoon when finger is drawn across, stirring constantly, about 10 minutes (do not boil).

💜 Strain through a fine mesh strainer into large bowl. Chill until cold, about 2 hours. Stir 1 c. whipping cream and chopped pistachios into custard.

💜 Process mixture in ice cream maker according to manufacturer's instructions. Transfer to container and freeze. (Ice cream can be prepared 3 days ahead.)

hot fudge sauce

3 Tbsp.	Butter, unsalted
½ c.	Water
⅓ c.	Heavy whipping cream
2 Tbsp.	Honey
8 oz.	Bittersweet chocolate, coarsely chopped
2 Tbsp.	Dark rum (optional)

PREPARATION

♥ Melt the butter in a medium saucepan.

♥ Add the water, cream, and honey and bring to a simmer over moderately high heat.

♥ Put the chocolate in a medium, heat-proof bowl and pour the hot cream mixture on top.

♥ Let stand until the chocolate melts, 1 minute, then stir until smooth.

♥ Stir in the rum.

Streetwalking

My father taught me how to walk—literally
and figuratively.

He did my daily exercises with me and helped me
regain whatever mobility I could after polio attacked
my right leg and hip.

But the walking that meant even more to me was
teaching me how to walk the streets of New York.
There is an 'art' to it, and my Dad had it down pat.

He would recite the final destination and then we'd
zig and zag, wending our way there.........watching the
traffic lights at the intersection ahead and deciding
whether to speed up or slow down to 'make the light'
if it was to our advantage, to 'cross' or stay on the same
side of the street. And at the next intersection, the
decision was made again.

In all the years I walked the streets of NYC with him,
I can't remember standing on a street corner waiting
for the light to change.

But I do remember stopping at one of the many
dairy restaurants in the Garment District to eat
potato pancakes, his second favorite food.

Perfect Potato Pancakes

perfect potato pancakes

Makes about 20 - 3" pancakes to serve 6

INGREDIENTS

3	Idaho Potatoes—large about 8 oz. each
1	Yellow onion, large, peeled
2	Eggs, large, lightly beaten
¼ c.	Flour—all purpose or matzo meal
2 tsp.	Kosher salt
	Freshly ground pepper, to taste
	Canola oil for frying

PREPARATION

💜 Using a 4 sided box grater, or the medium shredding disk in the food processor, grate potatoes alternately with onion.

💜 Place the shredded potatoes into a strainer above a large bowl, and with a wooden spoon, press out excess moisture. Transfer the potato mixture into another bowl.

💜 Carefully pour off the accumulated water in the first bowl and scrape the potato starch that remains in the bottom into the potato mixture.

💜 Stir the beaten eggs into the mixture and add enough flour or matzo meal to make a light batter.

💜 Add salt and pepper.

💜 In a large, heavy skillet, over medium-high heat, heat ½-inch of oil. Drop about 2 Tbsp. of batter into the oil and flatten a little. (The flatter the pancake, the crispier it will be.)

💜 Fry until golden brown, turn over and fry until browned.

   NOTE: Don't crowd them and don't turn more than once!

💜 Remove and drain on a wire rack.

💜 Keep warm in a 200 F oven on a cookie sheet.

chapter two

Preparation

The grandpa I knew

After her mother died, my mother's father lived with us in a small 1 bedroom apartment in Brooklyn. I was 2 when Grandpa Sam came and 5 when he left. I remember him being ill and my mother caring for him, my infant brother and me.

He was a sweet lovable man with a mustache and white hair. He was born in Russia and while I don't know how he earned a living there, in NYC he was a milliner, making beautiful hats in a factory on 37th Street. Among my most cherished possessions is a roll of pure silk ribbon from him.

I loved sitting on his lap and talking...and talking....and talking. Me talking, him nodding. One day, in order to stop my incessant chatter, he said he had something very important to tell me. I got very quiet. "Ina," he said, "everyone gets a certain number of words and when they use them up, they die."

I thought about that for a while, asked him how old he was, and then kept right on talking.

I would watch him eat a raw onion like it was an apple or he would butter some bread and lay a thick slice of onion on top. Despite the smell, I asked if I could have some. He showed me the hair on his chest and said that eating onions was the cause. I declined without hesitation.

Many years after he died I remembered the raw onion sandwich and made one. Of course I used the best pumpernickel, the best sweet butter and the juiciest Vidalia onion. And it was divine.

But I checked the mirror in the bathroom just to be sure.

A name on the door

I feel deeply connected to this grandfather I never knew. He died long before I was born and I was named for him, as is my cousin Ira. It is a Jewish custom to name newborns after the deceased, never the living.

What I know about my grandfather Isaac is that he was an early adopter of new technology since he was the first butcher shop in Philadelphia to have water-cooled coils in the meat lockers.

He gave great advice, which I have always followed: NEVER 'discount' your products or services. Give it away for good will, but never discount! He also said you could always trust a business when the owner puts his/her name on the door.

He was hardworking, connected to and respected in the neighborhood, and was a kind and generous man.

I grew up hearing about this wonderful man from my father, who missed him until the day he died.

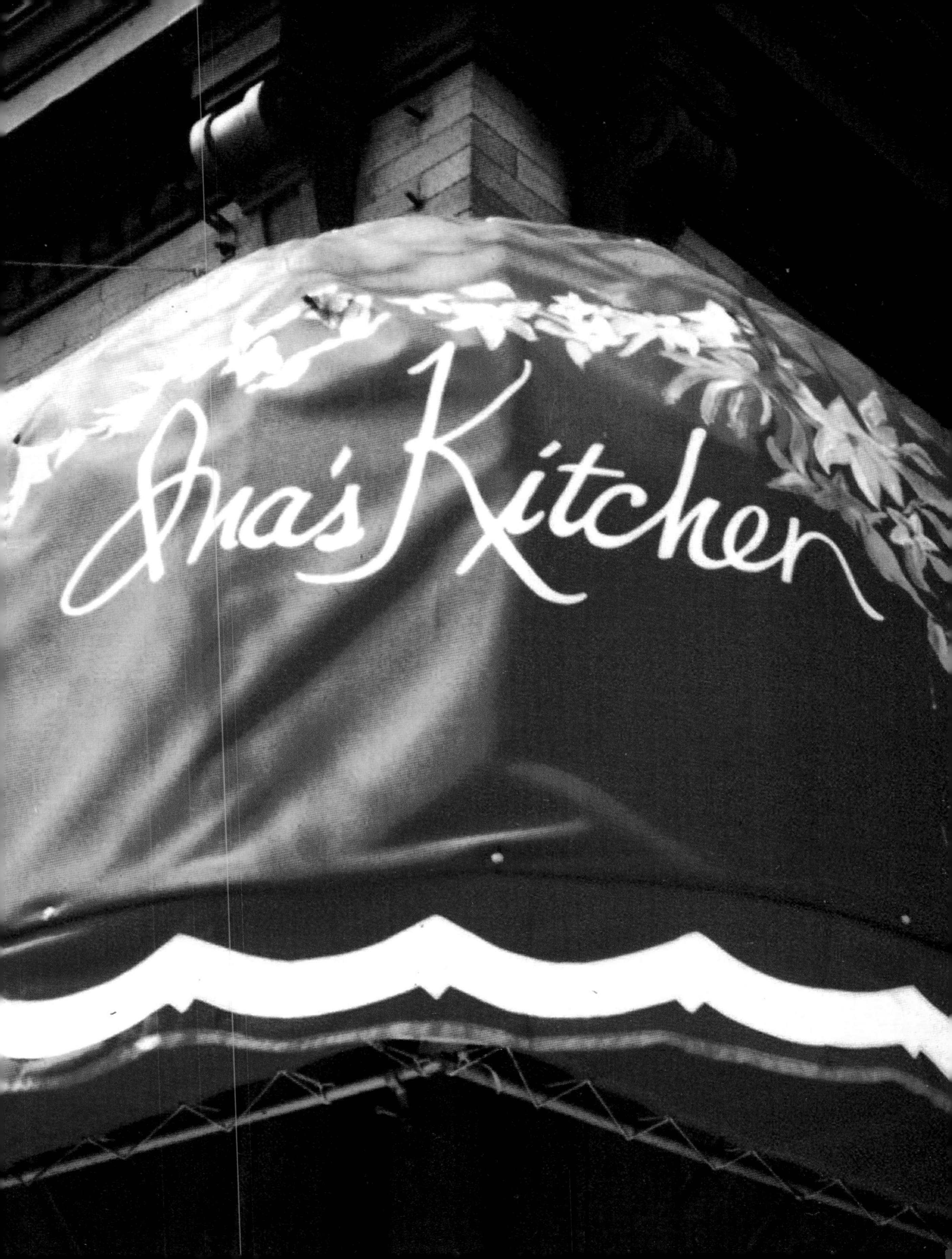
Ina's Kitchen

" *Where there is love there is life.* "

Gandhi

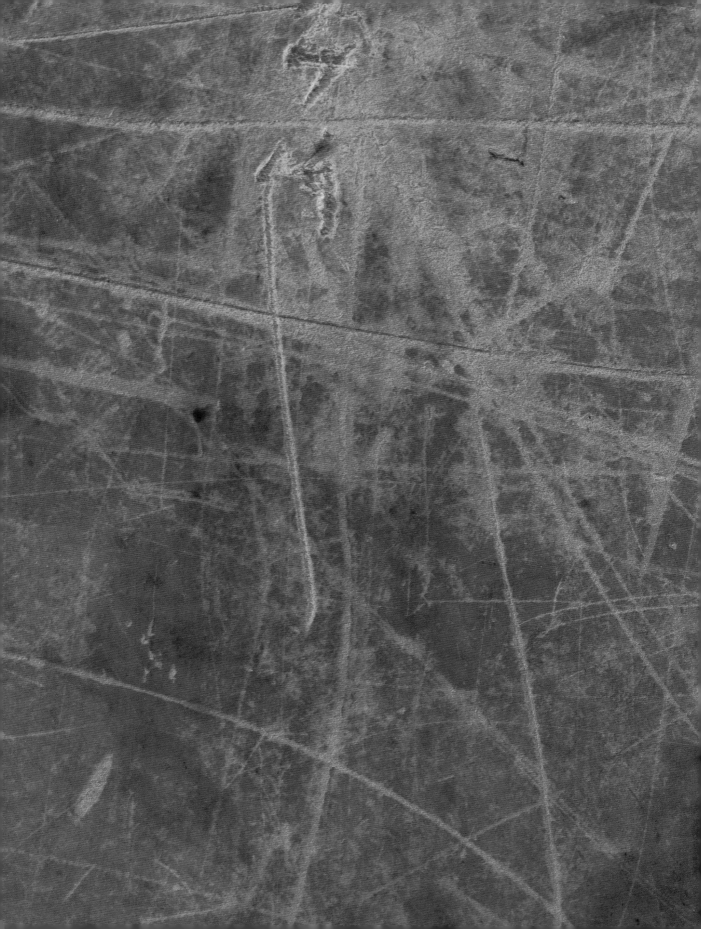

Recipe for life:

Fortune favors the brave.

Oy! it's an oyster!

One of the best jobs I ever had was working for George Lang, the genius behind the Café des Artistes and countless restaurant concepts around the world.

George asked if I would join him for a meeting at the Four Seasons restaurant to create a press luncheon for a Japanese company that was introducing a new whiskey which, up until then, had only been served in the Imperial Palace.

The limo drove us to that remarkable place where a Picasso tapestry hung, a reflecting pool was center stage in the dining room and the essence of power permeated the air.

We slid into a booth on the second level and I gulped at the realization that I was sitting next to George and across from Paul Kovi, the owner and Chef Seppi Rengli. These men were the royalty of the restaurant world in 1977.

We settled on a 3-course lunch, each course made with a different wine from the Japanese company. Chef suggested Oysters poached in champagne and 30 Herbs for starters. They all nodded and Chef ordered the dish from the server.

At that moment I stopped hearing anything else that was said. All I could think was, "I grew up in a Kosher home and I've never seen, touched or eaten an oyster. What do I do when the dish arrives?"

No amount of wishing kept that dish from the table. It arrived in a cast iron skillet filled with rock salt and seaweed decoratively woven under all 6 oysters.

They kept talking, I kept worrying.

Paul had one. George had one. Chef declined. To divert attention, I became engaged in the conversation, ignoring George's gesture to 'have one.' Finally, Chef held my gaze and said, "Please, I insist." Nowhere to run, nowhere to hide. And so I picked up the shell and ate the oyster.

With that first bite, I was hooked. The feel of the oyster in my mouth, the taste of the champagne butter sauce, redolent of garlic and herbs, was surprising and sensual and I was overcome with only one thought.....how could I eat the remaining 3 without anyone noticing?

$7.00 for lunch!

When we moved to Chicago in 1974, I was miserable and bereft. Commuter marriages weren't on the radar and wives followed husbands to new jobs/cities/lives and were expected to make a life for themselves. I had no family, no friends, no job and for months I was too sad to even try.

Bill was sympathetic but not much help. He did, however, give me a gift for our anniversary that, even though I didn't know it at the time, would have far reaching effects on me.

The gift was lunch, once a week, at Le Perroquet, the finest restaurant in Chicago. And in those pre-credit card days, he set up a 'House Account' so I could eat and sign the check. A 3-course lunch in this exquisite setting was $7.00. Extravagant to be sure!

I had a reason to dress up every Wednesday, take the bus to Michigan Avenue, stroll Walton Street, enter a beautiful old building and take the private elevator with the folding gate up to the restaurant where I was greeted by Jovan himself. I was taken to 'my' table at the turn of the banquette and settled in for a magnificent experience.

There was a ballet going on all around me, the staff in perfect synchronization. The hushed tones and the silent service all added to the mystique.

If ever a server, clearing a table, stacked a plate or put down a piece of flatware so that it was heard, he immediately turned toward Jovan who was already looking disapprovingly in his direction.

I took mental notes at each visit...notes I would recall when training staff at INA'S.

One perfect Spring day, the door at INA'S KITCHEN opened and Jovan appeared. I have never been as moved and terrified as I was at that moment. He said he came to pay his respects. I fed him, tried not to hover, listened for any clanging plates and generally trembled throughout his entire meal.

He called me over, pronounced breakfast the best he had ever had and said I should be very proud of what I had accomplished.

That wasn't my proudest moment, however.
My proudest moment was when he returned.

chapter three
Cooking

My first pancake—sort of

My mother was the kind of cook who washed each
bowl, utensil and pot as she used them so at the end
of a meal there were only a few plates to wash.
Her kitchen, like our home, was spotless.
("Oh, that Temmie Brody, you could eat off the
floor in her house.")

When I was in the 8th grade, my mother needed
surgery. Our suburban school was overcrowded so
we were on 'split session,' which meant I didn't begin
until 12:30 pm.

I organized the mornings, got my brother off
to the school bus, made the beds and cleaned up.

One morning a friend came over and I decided to
make pancakes, a task I had never undertaken
before. I can't remember where the recipe might have
come from or if there was a pancake mix in the house
(doubtful), but I do remember the growing stack of
pans in the sink as one by one I poured in the batter,
waited until I thought it was done and tried to turn it
over, watched it stick and then grabbed another pan
for yet another attempt.

As the time approached to leave for school, we still hadn't eaten a whole pancake, merely the partial pieces that we could un-stick. The literal piles of used and dirty dishes/pans/utensils were everywhere.

I did a mental calculation and after assuring myself that my mother was definitely NOT coming home unexpectedly 3 days after surgery, left a big note for my father who would be home early to visit her, apologizing and promising to wash everything as soon as I got home from school.

During the day I kept visualizing the mess I had left and worried about my father's reaction.

I raced home to find a clean kitchen, my father putting away the last pan. I held my breath, not knowing what to expect. He turned to me, laughing, and said, "I guess making breakfast isn't your strong suit!"

My, how things have changed!

foolproof pancakes

1 c.	Flour, all purpose
¾ c.	Buttermilk
¼ c.	Whole milk
1 tsp.	Sugar
½ tsp.	Baking soda
½ tsp.	Salt
1	Egg, large
2 Tbsp.	Butter, unsalted, melted

PREPARATION

💜 Combine ingredients JUST until moistened.
There will be LUMPS (that's a good thing).

💜 Heat a pan or griddle on high heat and brush with
oil to leave a thin film. Lower heat to medium.

💜 Pour ¼ c. of batter onto the pan or griddle
and wait for bubbles to appear.

💜 Turn carefully and cook for a few more minutes.
Serve immediately with pure maple syrup—just
like we do.

How it all began

I baked my first cake when I was 37 years old in 1980 when I had the idea for a surprise birthday cake delivery service—the obvious alternative to balloons, strippers and singers!

A tuxedoed 'butler' would deliver the cake, which had a sparkler on it, and read from a parchment scroll—the message written in calligraphy.

That fateful day, in *The New York Times Magazine*, there was a Craig Claiborne recipe for the first flourless chocolate cake I had ever seen. It was exactly the kind of cake I wanted to eat, but never having baked, it took 5 tries before it was close to the cake in the picture.

The delivery service was a great hit. I would bake the cakes at night, take them to my job (the last of the 21 I've had), and have 'at liberty' actors show up in tuxedoes and go off to deliver them.

That cake became THE cake for the delivery service since it was the only cake I had ever made. Then I got 'THE CALL' when someone asked if he could 'just order the cake!' That was the LIGHTBULB moment and THE DESSERT KITCHEN was born.

flourless chocolate cake

Preheat oven to 350 F.
Makes (1) 10" cake to serve 12-14.

INGREDIENTS

1 lb.	Butter, unsalted
1 lb.	Bittersweet chocolate, high quality, chopped
1 c.	Coffee, brewed and strong
8	Eggs, extra large, lightly beaten
1 c.	Sugar
1 Tbsp.	Vanilla

PREPARATION

💜 Butter the sides and bottom of a 10-inch springform pan and set aside.

💜 In the top of a double boiler combine the butter, chocolate and coffee and melt slowly.

💜 Stir occasionally until smooth.

💜 Remove from heat.

💜 In a mixing bowl, combine eggs, sugar and vanilla and stir until uniform.

💜 Whisk the egg and sugar mixture into the melted chocolate until combined.

💜 Pour the mixture into the prepared pan.

💜 Bake for 1 hour until the sides are firm and center barely jiggles.

💜 Cool on a wire rack until it reaches room temperature.

💜 Remove the side of the pan, cover with plastic wrap and refrigerate overnight.

The blobb

The 1980's seemed to spawn lots of 'gourmet brownies' like mint swirl, raspberry truffle and peanut butter chunk. Every flavor imaginable was loaded into that pure chocolate treat, rendering them unidentifiable as the revered American dessert.

As a backlash to the fad, I created THE BLOBB.... a mounded cookie/brownie with chocolate, walnuts, pecans, chocolate chips and 2 kinds of chocolate. When baked, they held the domed shape created by the ice cream scoop I used to measure them out. They became firm on the outside and amazingly soft on the inside.

They were the biggest selling item at The Dessert Kitchen and after the *New York Times* wrote glowingly about them, we began shipping them everywhere. We kept track and only missed Alaska and North Dakota!

After thousands and thousands of Blobbs, I got really tired of making them. Unable to find a production bakery that could meet my specifications, I decided to retire the recipe. It's the only recipe I haven't shared...........until right now!

They remain my most requested recipe and the customers who still ask get a glazed look in their eyes as they recall the experience of eating them. Yes, it was a treat that made hearts race and grown men beg!

There have been attempts to duplicate them but no one has come close. The *Chicago Sun-Times* tried and called theirs "Nearly Blobbs" but they weren't even in the same realm. Jill Van Cleave, in her wonderful book *Neighborhood Bakeshops* tried, but fell a little short.

I used to say, "There are only 3 things I don't share: Blame, Dessert and The Blobb recipe!" Now I'm down to just two.

They are a bit tedious to make, and you need a strong arm, but they are so worth the trouble! Freeze some in the unbaked state and each time you bake them off, you'll forget how much work you put into making them!

Blobbs

blobbs

NOTE: I've written this recipe differently because it requires more care to be sure they come out perfectly.

Preheat oven to 350 F.

INGREDIENTS & PREPARATION

4 oz.	Butter, unsalted
9 oz.	Dark chocolate (about 60%)
3 oz.	Unsweetened chocolate

♥ Melt slowly in a microwave or on stove top and cool to room temperature.

3 oz.	Flour, all purpose
½ tsp.	Baking powder
¼ tsp.	Salt

♥ Combine in a mixing bowl and stir vigorously. Set aside.

3	Eggs, large

♥ Put in a mixer and whip on medium-high speed until lighter and creamy.

1 ¼ c.	Sugar, superfine

♥ Add slowly to eggs and continue whipping until very light and creamy.

2 tsp.	Vanilla

♥ Add to egg mixture.

12 oz.	Chocolate chips
5 oz.	Pecan pieces
4 oz.	Walnut pieces

♥ Combine and set aside.

💜 When the egg mixture is ready, change the whip to a 'paddle' and gradually add the melted chocolate. Then add the flour mixture on low.

💜 Add the nut mixture and mix well. I finish by hand to be sure it's all combined at the bottom.

💜 Use a 2-inch ice cream scoop, packing mixture in and scraping off excess.

💜 Place mounds on a cookie sheet, lined with parchment or a silicone liner, about 2 inches apart.

💜 Bake at 350 F for 17-20 minutes.

💜 Tops should look a little dry and lighter in color.

💜 I also freeze the unbaked blobbs and bake them from frozen.

Recipe for life:

In true partnership, you show each other the possibilities, never the limitations.

Breakfast with Bill

Because my days in the storefront bakery stretched way into the night, the only time my husband and I could share a meal, catch up and connect was at breakfast. On the back door of our house was a list of 6 breakfast restaurants between home and the bakery. And each day it took a thoughtful moment to decide what we really wanted to eat.

If I wanted a great omelet there were two choices. If Bill wanted excellent pancakes, one. If we wanted really good coffee, there wasn't one (remember, this was the 80's when insipid coffee was the rule!). And so it went, day after day.

Sometime in the 10th year of the Dessert Kitchen, I remember saying out loud, "How hard can it be to make a great breakfast?" Maybe I had been asking the question all along, but it might have been the first time I got an answer from Bill. "You're the butter, flour, sugar and eggs expert. Aren't those the same ingredients we eat for breakfast?"
"So, what are you saying?" I asked. "Go for it!" he said. "Open a breakfast restaurant." And so I stopped kvetching and started dreaming.

When I think about The Dessert Kitchen, I remember long hours of silence partly due to the concentration needed to produce the same cakes over and over and partly because I worked alone for so much of the time. The sound of the mixers, the oven's fan and sometimes the phone were my companions. Rarely did I have music playing. I liked the focus to stay on my hands, which is probably why I don't have scars or burn marks after 11 years of baking! In that place, I began to understand the concept of 'zen.'

And so, while in my 'zen' baking state, I would visualize a restaurant, MY restaurant. I would see myself walking into a lovely quiet space, feeling welcome and acknowledged, being seated and looking over a menu that had many dishes I wanted to try. Unconsciously, I was building my dream from a guests' perspective.

I looked around and saw lots of formica tabletops at other breakfast places and white linens at the hotels. Service at the diner-type places was noisy and harried and at the hotels it was quiet and thoughtful, with the feeling of being on vacation.

I decided to go right between the two. I wanted the white tablecloths combined with moderate prices, a sense of neighborhood and, most of all, that 'vacation' feeling.

The menu would have unusual dishes with BIG flavors and, of course, the coffee would be perfect! Everything that was missing everywhere else would be a natural part of the INA'S experience.

Pasta Frittata

scones

Preheat oven to 350 F.

INGREDIENTS

2 lbs.	Flour, all purpose
¼ tsp.	Salt
¼ tsp.	Nutmeg
¼ c.	Baking powder
8 oz.	Butter, unsalted—cut into small pieces and frozen
1c.	Sugar
2 c.	Milk, whole
1	Egg, extra large

optional

1 c.	Raisins
	Melted butter for finishing

PREPARATION

- Put flour, salt, nutmeg and baking powder into a food processor and blend well.

- Add the butter and pulse 8-10 times.

- Add the sugar and process until uniform.

- Blend the egg with the milk.

- Add to bowl and pulse until mixture comes together.

- If using raisins, add now and pulse 1-2 times

- Turn dough out onto a floured surface and knead until smooth.

- Using a rolling pin, roll the dough until it is about ½-inch thick.

- Using a biscuit cutter, cut out scones and place on cookie sheet.

- Re-roll scraps gently and cut again.

- Brush tops with melted butter.

- Bake for 12-15 minutes, depending on size, until golden brown.

NOTE: Unbaked scones can be frozen.

chapter four
Serve and enjoy

ina's hot cocoa

INGREDIENTS

¼ lb.	Cocoa powder, very high quality
1 c.	Sugar
1 c.	Water, very hot

PREPARATION

♥ Mix ingredients until very smooth and store in refrigerator.

♥ When ready to use, combine 2 Tbsp. cocoa mix to 1 c. of whole milk and heat through on stovetop, in microwave, or with steaming nozzle of espresso machine.
Add more or less mix to your taste.

Recipe for life:

95% of life is asking for
what you want.

Dancing

In one of my newsletters I wrote about people
I wanted to feed. High on that list was Maria Tallchief—
an Oklahoma born Native American prima ballerina.

One of my favorite customers called to say she was
bringing Maria to lunch and when I sat across from
this icon, I told her why I wanted to meet her.

By the time I was 3, I was already angry about all the
pain and exercising that came with polio.

My mother took me to the Ballet Russe de Monte
Carlo in the hopes of inspiring me to keep exercising,
and when the curtain opened, I fell in love with the
Ballet and I fell in love with Maria Tallchief.

After that, when my father did my daily exercises with
me and I protested, he would quietly say,
"Maria Tallchief wouldn't say 'no,'" and I kept on.
Whatever mobility I regained was a direct result of her
name being spoken. I told her that story. And we both
cried. And then we ate.

I made her my Heavenly Hots Pancakes, which
are as light and elegant as her every move.

Maria Tallchief

heavenly hots

4	Eggs, large
2 c.	Sour cream, not Daisy brand
¼ c.	Cake flour
¼ c.	Potato starch
3 Tbsp.	Sugar
½ tsp.	Baking soda
½ tsp.	Salt

PREPARATION

💜 In a mixing bowl (or blender or processor), beat the eggs.

💜 Add the remaining ingredients and blend until smooth.

💜 Heat a non-stick griddle or fry pan on medium high heat.

💜 Coat with a thin film of oil.

💜 Carefully 'drop' a large spoonful of batter until it makes a circle of about 3 inches.

💜 When a few bubbles appear on the top, turn them over very carefully and cook until lightly browned.

💜 We serve them with a peach, raspberry, blueberry compote. I personally think maple syrup is too strong a flavor for them.

chapter five

Clean up

Recipe for life:

On an entrepreneur's top ten list of 'dreads,' death is not on the list... making payroll is.

What it meant to own ina's

What is it about restaurants that make otherwise sane people think they want to own one? For sure it's an 'adult phase dream,' since I never met a child who wanted to grow up and be a restaurateur! Is it that some of us make it look 'so easy' that everyone thinks they can do it?

We hear it all the time: "I love to cook and people tell me I should open a restaurant." "I throw a great party and really want to have my own restaurant."

I created a recipe for living that dream. Mine was more than counting money, schmoozing the customers, or having my name on the door. It was about creating an experience that respected the customer, the staff, the food and me.

I rarely get to cook anymore (or eat for that matter!), but I do get to watch people eat. It's very primal to feed people and bring them back to a memory. My food does that. So call it 'home cooking' or 'comfort food'—either one describes how I feel about feeding you.

And that recipe works every time.

ina

breakfast • lunch • dinner

1235 West Randolph Street
Chicago, Illinois 60607
312.226.8227
fax 312.226.5929
www.breakfast...

Recipe for life:

Practice being an expert in
'Plan B.'

The truth

Whatever your most magical fantasy is about owning a restaurant, it's true.

Regular customers, the backbone of any operation, come in and create the continuity. They bring family and friends, create, perpetuate and sometimes even 'make up' stories ("Didn't I see you on OPRAH?") and feel the pride in knowing 'the owner' who greets them like an old friend.

Others who have read about us or seen us on television seek us out and thrill at walking through the door, recognizing me or a familiar 'wall' or notice the unique salt and pepper shakers. Because our strategy is to make a new customer feel like an 'old' customer, they are greeted and made to feel welcome immediately.

Restaurants are the only retail situation where people come in to give you their hard-earned money. No one says, "Just browsing," or "Do you have that hamburger in blue?" It is because of this extraordinary trust that we feel the honor and obligation to give our best.

Yes, the farmers and vendors brought in new items and the kitchen was always trying to please me with a new salad or plating and the wine salespeople dropped off bottles of wine to taste, all of which were just perks. The real magic was the people who came to INA'S.

Every restaurant owner's dream is to open the door and have people walk through it. My dream came true every day.

That's the 'magical fantasy' part. The reality can be very different.

Does it sound like INA'S was a living, breathing entity? It was. And, as such, had all the problems of anything living. No one should ever be allowed to open a restaurant without a beginner's course in refrigeration, electrical, plumbing and sanitation. It's always the facilities management that's the dark side. As a business grows older, the building and the equipment also grow older, and less reliable. And, of course, there's always what life throws at us.

One beautiful summer Sunday morning I arrived to find my kitchen staff on the sidewalk instead of in the kitchen. The problem was all too obvious as I exited my car. In a brazen break-in, someone had driven a car through the windbreak AND the front door, destroying it, tearing it off its frame and leaving a mass of tangled wood and glass everywhere. I looked at the clock. One hour to opening.

I called the police, who did a sweep of the restaurant, let my bewildered cooks into the kitchen, gave out gloves from the winter 'lost and found' box, and everyone began hauling the wood pieces to the dumpster in the alley. We swept and vacuumed all the glass, carefully washed down the counter that would soon display baked goods and got ready emotionally, spiritually and physically to face the day.

Plan B.

Where our door had been was now a huge open entrance bringing in new light and 575 people that day....an all time record.

Another Sunday morning we arrived to find the compressor to the walk-in freezer blown. The food was still frozen solid but wouldn't be for long. We knew from experience that there's no place to buy dry ice on a Sunday in Chicago and you can't just go shopping for a compressor at 7 am.

Plan B.

We were 'lucky' that day because the wind chill was 20 below zero, so we emptied the outdoor laundry bin, washed and sanitized it, filled it with milk crates and loaded in all the food. Then we made the phone calls to our trusted repair people.

Then there was the time the kitchen exhaust hood stopped working an hour before a private party that was taking over the entire restaurant...a restaurant now filled with smoke.

Plan B.

Or when the dish machine died in the middle of a busy Sunday and we quickly reconfigured the dish area to hand wash, rinse and sanitize all the dishware.

Plan B.

Restaurants are theatre pieces and the guest in the chair is there with high expectations either from past visits or the stellar press we receive. The 'back of the house' was my worry and I wanted to make sure it never interfered with that experience.

Which brings me to what my real jobs were. The first was to fill the seats so that my staff earned a living. We participated in charity events; I spoke to any group that would invite me; I did cooking demonstrations on television and at events to generate press.

Because we were always searching for 'the next big/important trend,' we were way ahead of the curve—like leading the smoking ban with Dan Rosenthal and switching to trans fat-free oil and pasteurized shell eggs, all of which brought the press to our door.

I learned to be ready for an immediate response to the press as well: Frost in Florida and orange juice prices going up? Recall on peanut butter? Can we see your fried chicken? I was always ready with sound bites and an understanding of the reporter and cameraman's needs.

My second job was to metabolize anxiety. It wasn't my general manager's job to worry about that compressor or about payroll next week. It was mine. If anyone else was worried, then they couldn't and didn't do their best work.

Was it lonely? Sometimes. But my name was on the door and that is a source of never-ending pride and strength.

Recipe for life:

Set up everything within your power to succeed, turn your palms upward, take a deep breath and then let go.

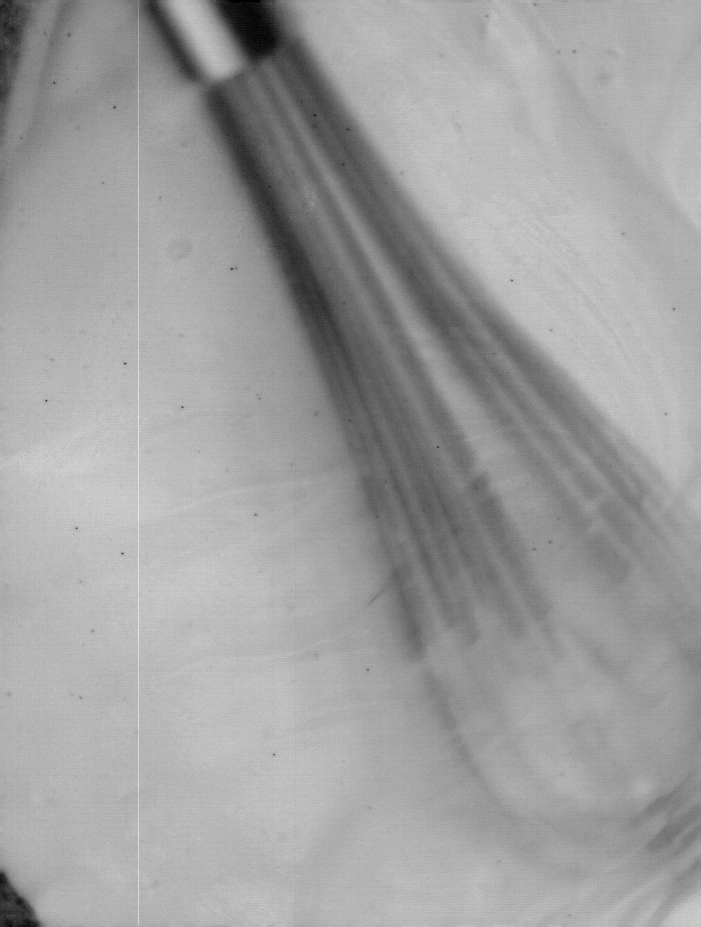

Ina's Recipes

spicy honey

12 oz.   Bottle Clover honey

1 ½ tsp.   "Vulcan's Fire Salt"
(*see note below*)

2 Tbsp.   Hot water—VERY hot

PREPARATION

- Pour out 2 Tbsp. honey from bottle, reserve for alternate use.

- Add Fire Salt to bottle.

- Add hot water and shake vigorously.

NOTE: *This incredible salt is available at* www.thespicehouse.com

135

ina's award winning fried chicken

INGREDIENTS

3 lb.	Chicken, organic or amish, cut into 8 pieces
3 qt.	Trans fat-free oil *(we use Canola for frying)*

Marinade:

2 qt.	Buttermilk
1 tsp.	Garlic powder
1 tsp.	Kosher salt
1 tsp.	Black pepper, freshly ground

Coating:

4 c.	Flour, all purpose
2 tsp.	Garlic powder
2 tsp.	Kosher salt
1 tsp.	Black pepper, freshly ground

PREPARATION

♥ Wash the chicken and trim any visible fat.

♥ Mix the garlic powder, salt, and pepper into the buttermilk.

♥ Put the chicken into a 1 gallon self-closing plastic bag and pour in the buttermilk.

♥ Close the bag, place on a cookie sheet or into a bowl and refrigerate for 2 hours or overnight.

PREPARATION

💗 Heat the oil in a heavy 6 qt. pot, over medium heat until it reaches 275 F, using a thermometer.

💗 For coating, combine flour, garlic powder, salt and pepper in a large mixing bowl.

💗 Remove breast pieces from marinade, shake off extra marinade and add breast pieces to coating mix.

💗 Dredge the breasts first and press the chicken into the flour mixture until well coated. Repeat with other parts.

💗 Shake off any excess flour. Re-dredge if any part is missing coverage.

💗 CAREFULLY AND SLOWLY put the chicken into the hot oil SKIN SIDE DOWN. It is best to start with the breasts and allow the oil to return to 275 F before adding thighs and legs. Add wings last.

Leave it alone (I'm not kidding!) for 10 minutes.
Then you can gently turn the pieces to keep them separate.

Cooking times:
Breasts: 20-25 minutes
Thighs: 18-20 minutes
Legs: 15-17 minutes
Wings: 13-15 minutes

💗 If you're not sure the chicken is done, use the tip of a sharp knife and poke to see if the juices run clear or use an instant-read thermometer, which should read 165 F.

💗 We serve our chicken with spicy honey and a waffle with real maple syrup, or with mashed potatoes and cole slaw.

ina's cole slaw

2 ½ lb.	Cabbage, green and red, thinly shredded
2	Carrots, shredded
2	Apples, Granny Smith, cored and thinly sliced
1 c.	Yogurt, plain, nonfat
1 c.	Hellmann's mayonnaise
¼ c.	Rice vinegar, unseasoned
1 tsp.	Dijon mustard
½ tsp.	Kosher salt, or more to taste
¼ tsp.	Black pepper, finely ground, or more to taste

PREPARATION

❤ Mix all ingredients thoroughly.

❤ Refrigerate for 2 hours. Taste just prior to serving and adjust seasoning.

❤ Serve well chilled. Garnish with chopped parsley or fresh chives if desired.

ina's potatoes

INGREDIENTS

2 lb.	Red potatoes, cubed
¼ c	Heavy cream
2 Tbsp.	Garlic, minced
2 tsp.	Kosher Salt
2 tsp.	Black pepper, freshly ground

PREPARATION

💜 Bring 6 qt. of lightly salted water to a boil.

💜 Add potatoes and cook for 10 minutes. Potatoes will be very firm.

💜 Drain potatoes, let cool to room temperature and then refrigerate until thoroughly chilled.

💜 Combine all additional ingredients with potatoes and refrigerate for at least 12 hours, mixing several times.

💜 Preheat oven to 425 F. Spread potatoes into a single layer on a rimmed baking sheet. Bake until golden brown and tender, 25 minutes.

Granola

granola

Preheat oven to 275 F.

INGREDIENTS

8 c.	Rolled oats, old-fashioned (see note)
¾ c.	Raw sesame seeds
1 ½ c.	Raw almonds, sliced
1 c.	Canola oil
¾ c.	Clover honey
2 Tbsp.	Nielson-Massey Vanilla Bean Paste
½ tsp.	Salt
½ c.	Raisins
½ c.	Dried cranberries

💜 In a large bowl, mix oats, sesame seeds and almonds.

💜 In a small saucepan, heat the oil, honey, Vanilla Bean Paste, and salt over low heat until honey is liquefied, stirring occasionally.

💜 Drizzle honey mixture over dry ingredients and stir until well coated.

💜 Spread evenly on 2 rimmed sheet pans.

💜 Bake in a preheated oven at 275 F for approximately 1 hour, stirring thoroughly and rotating pans every 15 minutes until well toasted.

💜 Remove pans and place on cooling racks.

💜 After oats are completely cool, add raisins and cranberries and store in an airtight container.

NOTE: Do not substitute quick or instant oats in this recipe.

ina's spinach

1 lb.	Spinach, frozen, chopped
1 tsp.	Fennel seed, freshly ground
2 tsp.	Garlic, freshly grated
¼ tsp.	Black pepper, freshly ground
¼ c.	Parmesan cheese, grated
3 Tbsp.	Olive oil, extra virgin
¼ tsp.	Kosher salt

PREPARATION

♥ Press spinach in a sieve until all liquid is removed.

♥ Thoroughly combine all ingredients.

♥ Chill for at least 1 hour to develop flavors.

♥ Use as an omelet filling or pizza topping.

chipotle mayo

INGREDIENTS

1 c.	Hellmann's mayonnaise
2 tsp.	Chipotle chile in adobo sauce
2 Tbsp.	Ketchup

PREPARATION

♥ Thoroughly blend ingredients with an immersion blender or in a small food processor for the best texture.

♥ Chill for 2 hours before serving.

Gingerbread
Pancakes

gingerbread pancakes

Yield: about 20 - 3" pancakes
Preheat oven to 200 F.

INGREDIENTS

Dry Ingredients

5 oz.	Flour, all purpose
½ c.	Sugar
½ c.	Potato starch *(see note on next page)*
1 oz.	Flour, whole wheat
1 tsp.	Baking soda
1 tsp.	Ginger, ground
1 tsp.	Cloves, ground
1 tsp.	Dry mustard
¼ tsp.	Pumpkin pie spice
½ tsp.	Salt

Wet Ingredients

2 c.	Buttermilk
½ c.	Sour cream
2	Eggs, large
¼ c.	Vegetable oil
2 Tbsp.	Molasses

PREPARATION

💜 Sift all dry ingredients together in a large mixing bowl and stir vigorously.

💜 Combine all wet ingredients and mix until well blended.

💜 Stir wet ingredients into flour mixture and blend well without overmixing.

💜 Heat non-stick pan or griddle over medium-high heat and brush with oil.

💜 Pour ¼ c. of batter onto the griddle for each pancake.

💜 Cook until bubbles appear on the tops—about 3 minutes. Turn over and cook about 1 minute more.

💜 Place pancakes, uncovered, on an oven-safe platter in the oven until all pancakes are made.

💜 I serve these with a lemon cream. Fold your favorite lemon curd into whipped cream until you reach your desired level of tartness.

NOTE: You can find potato starch (not flour) in a box in the Jewish food section of your supermarket. It might also be in the natural food area.

Moroccan Sweet Potato Stew with Raisins

black bean puree

1 can	Black beans, reduced sodium—28 oz.
2 Tbsp.	Canola oil
½ c.	Spanish onion, diced
2	Garlic cloves, grated
1 tsp.	Ina's Dirty Spice Mix (recipe, p163)
1 tsp.	Cumin, ground
½ tsp.	Oregano, dried
¼ tsp.	Paprika, sweet

PREPARATION

💜 Drain and rinse black beans.

💜 Heat oil in non-stick skillet over medium heat.

💜 Add onions and garlic and sauté until fragrant, but do not brown.

💜 Add spices and sauté for an additional 1 minute.

💜 Add black beans and simmer for 15 minutes over very low heat.

💜 Mash with a potato masher, or blend with a stick blender until desired consistency is achieved.

ina's dirty spice mix

Makes about ½ cup

INGREDIENTS

3 ½ tsp.	Paprika, ground
3 tsp.	Cumin, ground
2 tsp.	Thyme, dried
2 tsp.	Oregano, dried
3 tsp.	Dry mustard
4 tsp.	Kosher salt
4 tsp.	Black pepper, ground

PREPARATION

❤ Mix all ingredients thoroughly and store in tightly covered container.

Scrapple–
Ina's Version

scrapple—ina's version

Makes 12 servings

1 qt.	Water
8 Tbsp.	Butter, unsalted (1 stick or 4 oz.)
2 ½ tsp.	Salt
2 tsp.	Black pepper, freshly ground
¾ tsp.	Dirty Spice mix (p163)
1	Garlic clove, finely chopped
2 c.	Cornmeal, yellow
2 c.	Sharp cheddar cheese, grated
1 ⅓ c.	Frozen corn kernels, thawed
1 ⅓ c.	Black beans, canned, drained and rinsed

PREPARATION

💜 Bring to a boil water, butter, salt, pepper,
spice mix and garlic.

💜 Whisk in cornmeal until thickened, 3 minutes.
Reduce heat immediately or it will spatter dangerously.
When cornmeal is porridge thick, whisk in cheese.

💜 Remove from heat, switch to a heavy wooden
spoon and stir in corn and beans.

💜 Line a 9 x 5 loaf pan with plastic wrap.
Pack in the scrapple. Smooth the top. Cool to room
temperature and then cover and refrigerate overnight.

💜 Unmold scrapple by running a spatula around
the edges. Invert onto a cutting board and remove
plastic wrap.

💜 Cut into slices ½-inch thick. Crisp the slices in a
lightly oiled non-stick pan until golden on both sides
and heated through.

NOTE: The corn may pop and scorch the unprotected hand.

💜 Scrapple makes an excellent breakfast alongside
eggs and spicy sausage.

When I opened Ina's Kitchen 20 years ago, I knew I wanted an oatmeal flavored pancake to be on the menu along with traditional buttermilk and the magical Heavenly Hots.

These are the best because they are light, flavorful and are enhanced by blueberries or bananas and a small amount of Tim Burton's Maplewood Farms pure maple syrup.

Whole Wheat Oatmeal Pancakes

whole wheat oatmeal pancakes

Yield: 12 pancakes
Make ahead, needs overnight refrigeration

¾ c.	Old fashioned rolled oats (not quick cooking)
2 c.	Buttermilk, low fat
¼ c.	Whipping cream
1	Egg, large
2 Tbsp.	Sugar, brown
2 Tbsp.	Vegetable oil
½ c.	Flour, whole wheat
½ c.	Flour, all purpose
½ tsp.	Salt
1 tsp.	Baking soda
	Optional: 1-2 pints fresh blueberries or 2-3 bananas

PREPARATION

💜 Combine oats, buttermilk and cream in a bowl.
Cover and refrigerate overnight.

💜 The next day, combine the egg, brown sugar
and oil in a mixing bowl and set aside.

💜 In another bowl, combine flours, salt and baking
soda and stir vigorously.

💜 Add the oat mixture and the egg mixture to the
dry ingredients. Mix gently.

💜 Batter will be thick.

💜 Coat a large non-stick pan or griddle with
cooking spray. Heat to medium high.

💜 Measure ¼ c. of batter for each pancake
which will make them about 4 inches across.

💜 Cook for 3-5 minutes until tiny bubbles appear
and surface loses its sheen.

💜 Flip it over and continue to cook another 2-3 minutes
until cooked through.

💜 If adding blueberries or bananas, place them on pancakes
while first side is cooking. Add an additional 2-3 minutes
cooking time once you have flipped the pancakes to
ensure they are cooked through.

Baked French Toast

ina's bloody mary

46 oz.	Tomato Juice, Sacramento Brand
¼ c.	Lemon Juice
2 tsp.	Black pepper, coarsely ground
1 Tbsp.	Celery salt
1 Tbsp.	Horseradish, prepared
10 drops	Tabasco
8 dashes	Lea and Perrins Worcestershire sauce

PREPARATION

❤ Combine ingredients and stir or shake thoroughly.

❤ Refrigerate for 24-48 hours.

❤ Taste and adjust seasonings. Should taste highly seasoned.

❤ Fill a 16 oz. glass with ice, add 2 oz. (¼ c.) dill infused vodka or Absolut Peppar and then then top with bloody mary mix.

dill infused vodka

750 ml	Vodka, high quality
1 large bunch	Dill, fresh
1 medium	Red pepper, sweet, cored and quartered
3 small	Celery stalks with leaves

PREPARATION

- Combine all ingredients in a 1-liter glass carafe, ensuring that vegetables are completely submerged beneath the vodka.

- Cover and refrigerate for a minimum of 3 days and a maximum of 7 days.

- Strain vodka to remove vegetables and keep refrigerated for up to 3 weeks.

chicken pot pie

Makes 6 servings

PUFF PASTRY TOPS

NOTE: These tops can be made a day or two in advance. Cover loosely with plastic wrap and do not refrigerate. Reheat for a few minutes before serving.

1 sheet   Puff Pastry, store bought, 12 x 18 inches

PUFF PASTRY TOP PREPARATION

Preheat oven to 375 F.

- ❤ On a well-floured work surface, open the sheet of puff pastry and, using a rolling pin, roll it out until it is about 16 x 22.

- ❤ Decide in which dish/bowl you'll be serving the Pot Pie and using that dish/bowl as a guide, turn it upside down and cut out 6 rounds from the dough, using a sharp knife.

  (You can use the scraps and cut out leaves or even chickens!)

- ❤ Place rounds on a parchment lined baking sheet (or two) and with a fork, 'dock' the dough all over. That means make 'tracks' all over the pastry with a fork. This will keep the dough from puffing up.

- ❤ Bake at 375 F for 5-7 minutes or until medium brown. Remove from oven.

The Dessert Kitchen Recipes

Best Biscuits Ever

best biscuits ever

Preheat the oven to 375 F.
Line a baking sheet with parchment or a silicone liner.

INGREDIENTS

10 oz.	Flour, all purpose
1 Tbsp.	Baking powder
½ tsp.	Baking soda
¼ tsp.	Salt
1 Tbsp.	Sugar
4 Tbsp.	Buttermilk powder
4 oz.	Butter, unsalted, cut into pieces, frozen
1 c.	Water, ice cold

PREPARATION

💜 Into a food processor, put the flour, baking powder, baking soda, salt, sugar and buttermilk powder. Blend thoroughly.

💜 Add the butter and pulse 6-8 times and then run for 4 seconds more.

💜 Put the mix into a bowl and add the ice water. Stir gently, but thoroughly, until it forms a shaggy dough.

💜 Turn out onto a lightly floured work surface and knead about 10 times.

💜 Pat into a circle about 1-inch thick and use a 2-inch biscuit cutter to cut out biscuits.

NOTE: Use only a straight up and down motion…. never twist. Twisting the cutter may prevent biscuits from rising properly.

💜 Place on prepared sheet and bake for 12-15 minutes, until lightly browned. (Leftovers, if there are any, can be frozen.)

Advice and hints:

💜 I always keep weighed and portioned cut butter in containers in the freezer. ALWAYS.

💜 I use dried buttermilk powder, which you can find in the baking section. Since buttermilk usually comes in quarts, it always goes to waste. The powder keeps forever. Directions are on the canister.

💜 In order to be 'ready' for biscuit craving, I make the dry mix with the butter. Then I put the mix in a container in the freezer so all I have to do is add the cold water and bake!

Sour Cream Coffee Cake

sour cream coffee cake

(1) 9 x 13 pan
Preheat oven to 350 F.

8 oz.	Butter, unsalted and room temperature
2 c.	Sugar
4	Eggs, extra large
1 tsp.	Vanilla
1 lb.	Flour, all purpose
2 tsp.	Baking soda
2 tsp.	Baking powder
¼ tsp.	Salt
2 c.	Sour cream

TOPPING INGREDIENTS

1 lb.	Sugar, dark brown
1 ⅔ c.	Sugar, white
2 c.	Pecan pieces
5 Tbsp.	Cinnamon, ground

CAKE PREPARATION

💜 Using an electric mixer, blend the butter and sugar on medium speed until light and fluffy.

💜 Add eggs one at a time, blending well after each addition.

💜 Add vanilla.

💜 Combine the dry ingredients and stir vigorously.

💜 On a low speed, add the ½ flour mixture and ½ sour cream alternately until all is incorporated. Be sure to scrape the bottom of the bowl.

💜 Spray the pan with non-stick spray and carefully spread ½ the batter in the pan.

💜 Sprinkle ⅓ the topping onto the first layer of batter. Add remaining batter and smooth to cover. Sprinkle top with remaining topping.

💜 Bake at 350 F for 40-45 minutes or until a toothpick inserted into the middle of the cake comes out clean.

TOPPING PREPARATION

💜 Mix well and store in an airtight container.

Topping can be made in advance. Makes enough for 2–3 cakes.

The Perfect Cheesecake

the perfect cheesecake!

Preheat oven to 425 F.

1 ⅛ c.	Graham crumbs
2 Tbsp.	Sugar
¼ c.	Butter, unsalted, melted

1 ½ lbs.	Cream cheese, room temperature
1 c.	Sugar
3	Eggs, extra large
1 tsp.	Vanilla

CAKE PREPARATION

- Mix crust ingredients together in a bowl, pour into 9-inch springform, distribute evenly and press firmly into the bottom of the pan.

- In an electric mixer or processor, beat the cream cheese until smooth and add the sugar.

- Beat well and scrape the bowl to be sure all the cheese is incorporated.

- Add eggs, one at a time mixing until incorporated, then add vanilla.

- Beat until smooth.

- Pour into the prepared springform pan.

- Bake for 10 minutes at 425 F then lower oven temperature to 250 F and bake for 50 minutes.

- Cool to room temperature and then refrigerate overnight.

Variations:

To the basic cheesecake, add one of the following:

¼ c. mini chocolate chips

½ c. melted dark chocolate

1 c. pumpkin with 2 tsp. pumpkin pie spice

Ina's Cakey Brownies

ina's cakey brownies

(NOTE: there are two kinds of people in the world: fudgy and cakey. I'm a cakey!)

Preheat oven to 325 F.
Makes a half sheet pan: 12 x 18
(NOTE: I never make a small pan of anything! Since it's worth doing, I use a larger pan so I can freeze the remainder.)

Prepare the half sheet pan by lining it with foil. Grease the foil with a little oil.

INGREDIENTS

8 oz.	Butter, unsalted
¾ c.	Water, boiling
2 ¼ c.	Sugar
18 oz.	Chocolate (semi sweet, chopped)
1 Tbsp.	Vanilla *(NOTE: I use Nielsen-Massey Vanilla Bean Paste)*
¾ tsp.	Baking soda
¾ tsp.	Salt
6	Eggs, extra large
10 oz.	Flour, all purpose
12 oz.	Chocolate chips, semi sweet

PREPARATION

💜 Melt the butter (microwave or stovetop), add the boiling water and sugar and stir till dissolved.

💜 Put the 18 oz. of chopped chocolate, salt, vanilla and baking soda into a mixing bowl and pour the hot liquid over it.

💜 Let it sit for a minute and stir gently until chocolate is melted and smooth and cools down a little.

💜 Add eggs, one and time, mixing until incorporated.

💜 Add flour and mix briefly.

💜 Add the chips and stir to combine.

💜 Bake about 35-45 minutes, until center is puffed and toothpick comes out clean.

💜 Chill completely in pan.

💜 Peel off the foil and cut into desired sizes.

mocha mousse

½ c.	Sugar
1 tsp.	Instant coffee or espresso powder
½ c.	Water
6 oz.	Semi-sweet chocolate chips
2	Eggs, pasteurized
1 ½ c.	Heavy cream, whipped

PREPARATION

- Put sugar, coffee and water in a small saucepan and bring to a boil.

- Simmer for 3 minutes.

- Put the chocolate chips into a blender or processor and add coffee/sugar mixture. If using a blender, vent the lid and hold a towel over the vent to prevent splatter.

- Blend for 10 seconds.

- Add eggs and blend for 1 minute.

- Let cool for 5 minutes.

- Fold chocolate mixture into whipped cream gently but completely until mixture is no longer streaky.

- Pour into one serving dish or individual dishes and refrigerate.

- May be made the day before needed.

Vanilla Bean
Pound Cake

vanilla bean pound cake

Two things make this my new favorite pound cake:
I use a food processor and Nielsen-Massey Vanilla Paste.
Preheat oven to 350 F.

8 oz.	Butter (2 sticks) unsalted and melted in microwave or on stove top, cooled to room temperature
6 oz.	Cake flour (1 ½ c.)
1 tsp.	Baking powder
½ tsp.	Salt
8 ¾ oz.	Sugar (1 ¼ c.)
4	Eggs, large
1 Tbsp.	Nielsen-Massey Vanilla Paste

PREPARATION

- ❤ Preheat oven to 350 F and put oven rack in middle position.

- ❤ Grease a 9 x 5-inch loaf pan with butter and flour or non-stick spray.

- ❤ In a medium bowl, combine flour, baking powder and salt and stir vigorously. Set aside.

- ❤ In food processor, process sugar, eggs and vanilla for about 5 seconds.

- ❤ With machine running, and after stirring the melted butter well to mix in the separated solids, pour butter through feed tube in a very slow and steady stream.

- ❤ Turn the machine off when all the butter is incorporated.

- ❤ Spoon the flour mixture on top of the egg mixture and pulse a few times until you see it disappear.

- ❤ Scrape the flour from the edges and pulse a few more times.

- ❤ Pour batter into prepared loaf pan.

- ❤ Bake for 15 minutes at 350 F.

- ❤ Lower oven temperature to 325 F and bake until deep golden brown and tester comes out clean.

- ❤ It should bake about 35-40 minutes.
  (Rotate pan halfway through the baking time.)

- ❤ Cool in pan for 10 minutes.

- ❤ Unmold and let cool completely on a wire rack.

fruit crisp topping

7 oz.	Flour
4 oz.	Sugar, white
4 oz.	Sugar, light brown
½ tsp.	Cinnamon
½ tsp.	Nutmeg
6 oz.	Butter, unsalted, cut into small pieces and chilled
	Your favorite fresh fruit

PREPARATION

- Put all dry ingredients into a food processor and combine.

- Add butter and 'pulse' 7-10 times until the butter pieces are quite small—about the size of rice.

- Store the topping in an airtight container in the refrigerator.

TO BAKE CRISPS
Preheat oven to 350 F.

- Fill 8 oz. heatproof ramekins with blueberries, pitted apricots, or pitted Italian plums and put ¼ c. of topping on each.

- Place ramekins on a baking sheet lined with parchment, foil or a silicon mat.

- Bake the crisps at 375 F for 15-17 minutes until fruit is bubbling and topping is golden brown.

- Allow to cool for 5-10 minutes before serving as the baked fruit will be very hot.

Chocolate
Souffle Cake

chocolate souffle cake

Yield: (1) 9" round cake to serve 10
Preheat oven to 350 F. Line a 9" springform with parchment.

CAKE INGREDIENTS

9	Eggs—large, separated
1 c.	Confectioners sugar
½ c.	Cocoa powder, unsweetened
1 tsp.	Vanilla
½ tsp.	Cream of tartar

FILLING/FROSTING INGREDIENTS

4 c.	Whipping cream—cold
½ c.	Confectioners sugar
¼ c.	Cocoa powder, unsweetened

CAKE PREPARATION

- In a bowl of electric mixer, combine yolks with confectioners sugar and cocoa powder.

- Beat until thick and lightened in color.

- Add vanilla and set aside.

- In a clean bowl with a clean whip, beat egg whites until frothy and large bubbles appear around the edge. Add cream of tartar and increase speed until the whites are thick and glossy. (To test, tilt the bowl. If the whites slide, they need a little more beating.)

CAKE PREPARATION

- Mix a large spoonful of whites into the chocolate mixture to 'lighten' it.

- Gently fold whites and chocolate together.

- Carefully pour into prepared parchment-lined springform pan.

- Bake at 350 F for 35-40 minutes. When you remove the cake from the oven, it will be a rounded cake. As it cools, the center will sink.

- Cool on a wire rack.

- When completely cool, remove from pan by carefully loosening the edges with a metal spatula. Gently place a plate on top of the cake and invert. Remove parchment from bottom of cake and place on serving platter right side up.

FILLING/FROSTING PREPARATION

- Chill the bowl and beaters.

- Mix all ingredients together on low speed.

- Scrape the bowl and increase speed.

- Scrape the bowl again to be sure all ingredients are mixing.

- Increase speed and beat until beaters leave a definite imprint in the whipped cream.

- Spread filling smoothly over top and sides of cake.

- Decorate with shaved white or dark chocolate or sprinkles.

- Keep refrigerated until ready to serve.

Carrot Cake

carrot cake

Makes (1) 9" two-layer cake
Preheat oven to 350 F.

CAKE INGREDIENTS

4	Eggs, extra large
2 c.	Sugar
1 ½ tsp.	Salt
1 ½ tsp.	Baking soda
2 tsp.	Baking powder
2 Tbsp.	Cinnamon
1 ½ c.	Canola oil
14 oz. can	Carrots, drained and pureed
14 oz. can	Pineapple, crushed, drained
1½ c.	Flour
½ c.	Currants

FROSTING INGREDIENTS

24 oz.	Cream cheese, room temperature
1 ¼ c.	Confectioners sugar

CAKE PREPARATION

- In a large bowl, beat eggs and sugar until thick and creamy.

- Add salt, baking soda, baking powder, cinnamon and oil and beat until well blended.

- Add carrots and pineapple and mix well.

- Add flour and mix well.

- Add currants and mix gently.

- Coat each 9-inch round pan with non-stick spray.

- Divide the batter evenly and bake for 45 minutes or until top springs back when gently touched.

- Let cool completely in the pan.

FROSTING PREPARATION

- In a medium bowl, beat the cream cheese until light and fluffy.

- Gradually add the confectioners sugar.

- If the mixture is too soft to use, cover and refrigerate for an hour.

- Put the remaining frosting on top of the cake and swirl it a little to give it a finished look.

ASSEMBLY

- Turn out the first layer onto a plate. Use half the frosting and just cover the layer.

- Put the remaining layer just on top of the frosting, being careful not to press it down to hard. The frosting should not come out the sides.

- Put the remaining frosting on top of the cake and swirl it a little to give it a finished look.

ina's favorites

Smoque BBQ's Smoked Brisket and Pulled Pork
www.smoquebbq.com

Burton's Maplewood Farm Maple Syrup
www.burtonsmaplewoodfarm.com

National Pasteurized Eggs
www.safeeggs.com

Chicken Sausage by Amylu
www.atkfoods.com

Paulina Market
www.paulinameatmarket.com

Jones Farm's Cherrywood Smoked Bacon and Ham
www.jonesdairyfarm.com

Heartland Meats Hamburger
www.heartlandmeats.com

Intelligentsia Coffee
www.intelligentsiacoffee.com

Labriola Harvest Twists and Ciabatta
www.labriolabaking.com

Nielsen-Massey Vanilla Bean Paste
www.nielsenmassey.com

Vulcan's Fire Salt
www.thespicehouse.com

Seedlings Fresh Fruit
www.seedlingfruit.com

Scooter's Frozen Custard
www.scootersfrozencustard.com

Wholesale Wines
www.H2vino.com

Chicago Green City Market
www.greencitymarket.org

Who's Hungry Magazine
www.whoshungrymag.com

Les Dames D'Escoffier
www.lesdameschicago.org

The Future

Recipe for life:

Never grieve until
the day you have to.